PIDGIN TO DA MAX
HANA HOU

Conceived and Written
by

DOUGLAS SIMONSON
KEN SAKATA
PAT SASAKI
TODD KUROSAWA
AND ALL THE FOLKS
ON THE BACK COVER OF THIS BOOK

With a special MAHALO to
KREGG LUKE

Illustrated
by
DOUGLAS SIMONSON

With the assistance of
TODD KUROSAWA
ANGIE ACAIN

Design and Layout
by
PAUL S. OTAGURO

3565 Harding Avenue
Honolulu, Hawai'i 96816
phone: (808) 734-7159
fax: (808) 732-3627
e-mail: sales@besspress.com
http://www.besspress.com

This book is dedicated to
ALL
the people of Hawaii.

The authors wish to thank and acknowledge the following people and groups for their support of, and belief in, this project.

Chester Akamine; Aku; Allen, John and Lei--Bank of Hawaii Waiakamilo; Pat Banning; Pierre Bowman; Andy Bumatai; Don Chapman; Randy Chun; The Clients Corporation; Evelyn DeCastro; Graphic Prep, Inc; Harris nd Smith; Garrick Higuchi; Leland and Pat Johnston; KGMB-TV and the Crew of Hawaii Moving Company; KCCN; KITV; Bill and Bobbie Kikuchi; Victoria Lam; Stuart W. Lesses; Steve Miller; Collin Miyabara; Wayne Miyaji; Paul and Susan Otaguro; Salu Reid and the Amerika Samoa Office/Hawaii; Herman and Lillian Sakata; Randy Sasaki; Richard, Aileen and Laura Sasaki; Virginia Stein; Tom and Barbara Takata; Barbara Tong; Tongg Publishing; Holly and Doug Worrall; Claire Zukeran.

CREDITS: Layout and Design, Paul Otaguro; Typesetting and Photography, Graphic Prep, Inc; Printing, Malloy Lithographing.

INTRODUCTION

Just in case you've been out of the state for a while, our first book, PIDGIN TO DA MAX, has become a publishing phenomenon. At this writing we have printed 200,000 copies--and you folks are still buying it!

That's exciting for us, because we had a hard time getting PIDGIN TO DA MAX published in the first place. Everybody said you can't even break even on something like that. They said that doing something just for local people doesn't make sense. But we were stubborn. We really believed that it was time for a book *just* for local people. The sales of the book have shown we were right.

It's exciting to be the creators of something so successful. But what's much nicer is the response we've gotten from the folks who have read PIDGIN TO DA MAX. We've gotten all kinds of letters --even some pilau ones--but hundreds of letters thanking us, telling us how much PIDGIN TO DA MAX has been appreciated. And telling us about some of the words we left out of the book.

We started planning PIDGIN TO DA MAX HANA HOU! almost as soon as the first book came out. We didn't know it was going to be so easy to write. But with all the words YOU have been sending us, the book was practically written before we started! All we had to do was choose the words we wanted to use in this book. Because, would you believe it, we still have several hundred words and expressions we haven't used yet!

Without these contributions, you wouldn't be holding this book in your hand right now. We feel it's important to acknowledge the many, many contributors to this book. That's why we listed them on the outside of the book. There were lots of others who wrote to us, too, and this book is really an expression of aloha e mahalo to ALL of those people.

So listen--dis book ju' li' da las' one, yeah? We had good fun writing 'um, and we hope you have good fun reading 'um! 'An' remembah, like we went tell you las' time, we no like insult anyody. . . we jus' like TEASE! (We lita' bit kolohe, you know.)

We hope dis book going make you BUS' LAUGH!

Aloha,
PEPPO
KEN
PAT

A WORD OF CAUTION TO THE NON-LOCAL

If you don't already speak pidgin, you might need some help from local friends to understand this book. Remember, PIDGIN TO DA MAX is not a tourist guide to pidgin. So don't try to speak it after reading this book. You'll just get into trouble.

AHANA, AHANAKUKULANA
(a ha na koo koo LAH na)
Ahanakokolele.

AI KA PRESSURE! (eye ka PRESHAH)
No can handle!

AI KA PRESSURE!

AI-SOS (eye SOHSS) Sound of Filipino praying. Also AI-ZOOS.

AITAE (EYE tie) Samoan word meaning "I am going to kill you soon."

AIYAH! (eye YAH) Oh wow! Oh my goodness!

ALAS, AALAS (AW lahz, ah AH lahz) Pau; no mo'; all gone. "Aalas dollahs" means no mo' kala.

ALL JAM UP See JAM UP.

ALU-ALU (ah loo AH loo) Loose, baggy — like surfer shorts.

ANO AI (ah no EYE) Hawaiian for "Have a nice day."

APURUPANTSU (ah poo doo PONCE oo) Old-kine Japanese pidgin for apron-pants coveralls.

'ASS RIGHT You are correct. "Wot, t'ink you rough?" "ASSRIGHT! Why, boddah you?"

ATSUI (ot SOO ee) Hot. Or, Hot Stuff.

ATTITUDE

ATTITUDE When somebody tink deir fut no smell, dey get plenny attitude.

AUWE (ow WEIGH) What you say when someone takes your parking space.

BABA STRIKE Used in the days when long hair was not accepted.

BABOOZE (bah BOOZE) Portagee word for clown or dummy.

BALL HUGGAH Shorts or swimtrunks two sizes too small. "What, Aaron . . . you t'ink you macho when you wear dose ball huggahs?"

BACHI (BAH chee) Japanese curse. When you do something rotten and nasty, going come back to you, brah!

BAMBULA
(bom BOO la)
Another word for
BAMBUCHA.

BEFO' TIME
Long time ago;
way back.

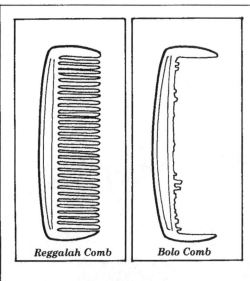

Reggalah Comb   *Bolo Comb*

BOLO No mo' hair.
Short for BOLOHEAD.

BOY-FLOWER
Anthurium.
No comment.

BUCKALOOSE To break away, to bust loose.
"Hahd, but! My kite wen buckaloose!"

WHAT, MOKI—RODNEY-BOY WEN *BUCKALOOSE* AGAIN?

BUCKALOOSE

BUFO (BOO fo) Local insect exterminator.

BULL Head tough guy. See also TRUE BOOL.

BUS' 'UM OUT No hide! Share 'um!

BUS' FAYACRACKA What you do on New Years Eve. Or whenevah you get excuse.

BUS' LAUGH So good fun you stay rolling on da floor. Like when you reading dis book, yeah?

BUS' NOSE Reaction to extremely bad breath. "Wow, Bernice, BUS' NOSE! Whatchoo had fo' lunch?"

CAN SEE DA HANAKUSO No gimme attitude, Miss Hi-Maka-Maka.

CANNERY, DA Last-resort summer job.

DA CANNERY

CAP Short for CAPILLARY. Nickname for somebody just aching to bleed. "Ey, what, cap, you like beef o' wot?"

CATCHING T'RILLS

CATCH T'RILLS Like one teenager looking pilau pictures first time.

CHALANGALANG (cha LANG ah lang) Da kine Hawaiian music. Sounds like the word.

CHARGE 'UM

CHARGE 'UM! When you want something so bad you jus' go fo' broke. Like when you at one disco and you attack da haole chick fo' go dance.

CHANG Pake so tight even da pakes tink he tight.

CHEW BEEF What happens when you get your pants caught in the chain of your bike.

CHEW BEEF

CHICKEN FAT Gotta get up when half-asleep an' listen to dat corny song an' do jumping jacks an' bicycles an' all kine junk stuffs.

CHICKEN FAT

CHOKE (1) Plenty. "Wow, get choke pakalolo until Green Hahvest!" (2) No can handle. "Da quarterback when choke, ass why dey lose."

COURICHE (koo DEESH) Portagee swearword.

DOUBLE EYES Gotta use plenny mascara, uku long false eyelashes, an' scotch tape. Or if you rich, get da operation.

 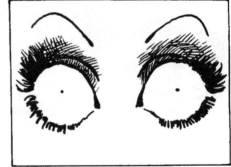

Befo'   **DOUBLE EYES**   *Aftah*

DOUBLE LUNCH Go back for seconds da first time.

DRY-LAND KUMU What you catch on Kalakaua Avenue.

DRY-LAND KUMU

DRY, SOME DRY, DRY EGGS (1) When da joke not funny. (2) One guy who no like participate in da fun.

DRAPES
Bell bottoms.

DRAPES

EAT IT To fall down, get in one accident, get totalled.

EE-HAH (eeeeeeeeee HAAAAAAAAAA) Expression of enthusiam.

EY NE! HEY YOU!

FBI Full-Blooded Ilocano.

FA-OOGA FACE (pronounced like it looks)
Japanese girls who wear real packed-on makeup an' eyelashes out to heah an' real red lipstick.

FA-OOGA FACE

FA'AFETAI (fa ah fay TIE) Samoan fo' T'ANKS EH?

FA'AMOLEMOLE (fa ah mo lay Mo lay)
Samoan for PLEASE. A good word to know.

FAH-OUT Far out.

Haole   *FAH-OUT*   Local

FATTABULL (fah tah BOOL) Beeg buggah.

FIGGA

FIGGA (FEE gah) Haole: "That makes no sense to me." Local: "How you figga?"

FIGHT RUBBAH Game where you shoot each other with knotted rubber.

FO'-WHEELAH

5-4-4 (fi fo fo) If you can count in Japanese, you know this means to go to the bathroom.

FO'WHEELAH Four-wheel drive. Two wheelah is reggalah cah.

GALA-GALA, GULLA-GULLA Mucus in yo' t'roat. Also GALAS.

GANGY, GANGIES (GANG gee) Da gang. "See you laytah, gangies!"

GETCHO' RAGS

GETCHO' RAGS Time of the month. Haole: "You're certainly in a good mood today." Local: "Wow, getcho' rags o' wot?"

GIRI-GIRI

GIRI-GIRI (giddy GIDDY) Cowlick. Da place where two-t'ree hairs always stick up no mattah what you do.

GO FO' BROKE Like when you standing on top of a steep, dried-out canal wit' yo' skateboard an' everybody scared, but one guy says, "Ey, we go fo' broke!", an' you chance 'um.

GO STAY GO Used in many ways: GO STAY GO, GO STAY WAIT, TRY GO STAY WAIT, GO STAY TRY, GO STAY COME, an' li' dat.

GO STAY GO

NOW WHY DID YOU ASK ME TO COME OVER HERE AND SEE YOU, AND AS SOON AS I GET HERE, YOU GET UP AND LEAVE?!

HOWCUM I GO STAY COME AN' YOU GO STAY GO??

Haole

Local

Haole   *GOING GO*   *Local*

GOING Encouragement. "Should I tank dis beer o' wot?" "Going, brah, going!"

GOING GO Future tense of GOING. "Bambai I going go."

GUNFUNIT (gun FUN it) Confound it! Also GUNFUNIT, YOU!

HABUTS (ha BOOTS) To be real upset. To have a tantrum. Also HABUTERU.

HAGEMOGI (Hay gay MOE ghee) Rotten teeth.

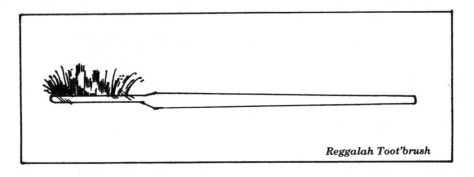

Reggalah Toot'brush

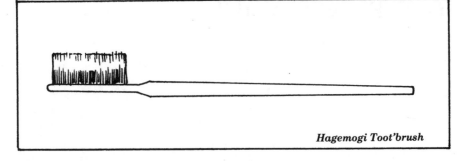

Hagemogi Toot'brush

HALA

HALA (ha LAAAAAHHHHHH) Shame, shame, SHAME on you!

HANAKOKOLANI Yet another way to say AHANAKOKOLELE.

HANAPA'A Working really well.

HANAPA'A

HAPA HAOLE (hop a HAOLE) Product of interracial meeting. "Him hapa, yeah?" "Yeah, his faddah from Chicago an' his moddah from Manila."

HAUNA PILAU (how nah pee LAU) Smell so bad you cannot even describe it. Words cannot do it justice.

HEAVIES Heavy-duty. "Wow, yo' cah only heavies!"

HIGH WATERS Short pants or long shorts. Also FLOODS.

HIGH WATERS

HO! Japanese pidgin exclamation used before any very emotional statement. Example: "Ho, da waves was pumpeen yestaday!" Often used before DA BUGGAH.

Haole

Local

HOD-ICE Ice cake. Homemade popsicles.

HOD-ICE

HOLD ASS When you going 70 miles an hour and somebody pull in front of you and slow down and you come so close to creaming 'em, dass when you hold ass. Especially when you get one new cah.

HONE-HONE (ho nay HO nay) Another word for HUM SUP.

HOOMALIMALI (ho oh mah lee MAH lee) Laying it on pretty thick.

HULI HULI CHICKEN

HULI HULI CHICKEN What you do with the loser from the cockfight.

HULI MAKA HULI

HULI MAKA HULI (hoo lee mocka HOO lee) Dry-land wipeout.

HUM HA BREATH Seafood version of KIM CHEE BREATH.

HUM SUP Chinese for MANE'O.

HUNDRED PERCENT What a babooze doesn't have. "He not hundred percent."

ICHIBAN (ee chee BON) Numbah one.

IGOROT (ee go DOTE) Very insulting thing to call one Filipino.

IGOROT

INTENSE

INDAI (een DIE) Sweetheart from Waipahu.

INTENSE Heavy-duty to da max.

ITAI (ee TIE) Soah.

JAM UP (1) Messed up. "You know Bill, he wen eat it into da reef an' now his face stay all JAM UP!" (2) Hemajang to da max. Freeway on Friday afternoon good example.

JOONYA/JAMMING/JAP SLAPS

JAMMER One real cool, well-respected guy. When he goes for something, he gets it.

JAMMING Da bes', da greates'. "Wow, JAMMING da grinds! Us go scahf 'um!"

JAP SLAPS (1) Punishment you get from your Japanese teacher. (2) Flipflops.

JOONYA (JOON yah) Junior-boy.

JUNK AN' A PO How you flip coins when
you small-keed time an' you no mo' coins.

JUNKALUNKA (junk ah LUNKAH)
Pakajunk.

JUNKEN A MUNKEN,
A SUCKA SUCKA PO,
WAILUKU WAILUKU,
BUM BUM SHOW
Kids' way of deciding who goes first.

Also
JUNKEN A MUNKEN,
A SUCKA SUCKA PO,
WAILUKU WAILUKU,
BIG FAT TOE.

JUNKEN A MUNKEN...

KAKA LIMU
(ka ka LEE moo)
Another way to say
MOE LEPO.
Also means NOTHING.
"What you caught
today?" "Kaka limu,
brah, kaka limu!"

KALAKOA (ka la KO ah)
Plenny colors all
hemajang.

KALAKOA

KAMABOKO SLIPPAHS

KAMAAINA (comma EYE nah) Word used only by haoles to denote a longtime haole resident. Also used to mean a discount applying only to locals. "SPECIAL KAMAAINA RATES!"

KAMABOKO SLIPPAHS (comma BO ko SLEE pahz) Flipflops, but thick like fishcake.

KAPU (ka POO) (1) Forbidden. "No go ovah deah, dat place kapu." (2) Reserved. "Who wen cockaroach da orange juice from da icebox aftah I wen kapu 'em? I going kill da buggah!"

KAPULU (ka POO loo) Messy, sloppy.

KARAI (ka DIE) Spicy, hot, like chili peppah. KARAI WATER: Chili pepper water.

KAPULU

KARAI

KEKEFACE

KARANG (ka RANG) To twist, hit or nail. Often used with YO' ALAS.

'KAY FINE DEN! "All right already! Have it your way! Last t'ing I saying to YOU!"

KEIKI (KAY kee) Hanabata kid. Like Melveen says, "Do it fo' da keikis!"

KEKE (KAY kay) (1) All drunk, loaded. (2) Pimples.

KEKEFACE Uku million zits.

KICK OUT Getting off the board before you fall off. Sort of like quitting just before you get fired.

KILL FIGHT Killjoy. Somebody who like rain on yo' parade.

KILLAH WHIFFAH (kee lah WEE fah) Heavy fut fumes.

KOLOHE

(ko LO hay) If Dennis the Menace was one Hawaiian. . . also means real mane'o, real naughty, but sexy.

HO, GERALD! KILLAH WHIFFAH!

KILLAH WHIFFAH

KOMPA (COMB pah) To share, be partners with. Haole: "Let's combine our funds so that we can make this purchase."
Local: "Us go kompa kompa, brah!"

KONA WEATHER, KONA WIND Hauna weather.

KOOLS State Cigarette of Hawaii.

KUKAE IN DA EYE Offerings from da sky.

LACK (1) No class. (2) Broke; no mo' kala. (3) Jus' no mo' notting at all.

LACK

Speech bubble: WOW BRAH, YOU WEN *LAWN MOWER DA LAWN* O' WOT??

LAWN MOWER DA LAWN
(1) To mow.
(2) To cut anything.

LAWN MOWER DA LAWN

LI HING MUI Pake munchies dat give you cho cho lips.

LIKE MEDAL? See SO? T'ROW PAHTY?

LILIBIT (LILLAH bit) Not much.

LITTLE TOKYO Makeenley High.

LOBSTER SKIN Broiled shahkbait.

LOCAL STYLE (continued) The way guys hang their arm outside the car when driving. The way people use their whole bodies when talking.

LOCO-MOCO One local food with rice, hamburger patty, fried egg, and gravy on top. (Sometimes when you not looking they throw in spam instead of the hamburger.)

LOCAL STYLE

LOSE 'UM Make ass to da max. "I was so buss up, I wen LOSE 'UM!"

LUMPY GRASS Da kine spring-action grass. Popular with people who no like mow da lawn. Also POKI-POKI GRASS.

LUNA (LOO nah) Boss.

MAIKA'I (my KA'ee) Fine, well, good.
"Pehea oe?" "Maika'i fine!"

MAKAPIAPIA (ma ka pee ah PEE ah)
Glue factory in da eyes. Also PIAPIA.

MAKE DOG MOUT'
Morning breath.

MAKE DOG MOUT'

MAKE HOUSE Make yourself at home; move in like you own the place. What visiting mainland relatives sometimes do.

MAKE SHIBAI (shee BUY) What Japanese politicians do right before election. That's the only time they talk.

MALIHINI
(molly HEE nee)
What you find
inside tour buses.

MALIHINIS

MAMA-SAN
Local Japanese for AUNTIE.
Also used to mean someone who acts like one but isn't old enough yet.

MAMA-SAN

MANAPUA MAN (ma na POO ah) Smallkeed time when you heah him coming an' you run to yo' moddah fo' one quartah.

MANGO SEASON

MANGO SEASON Summahtime.

MAP HANG (1) Expression of sadness or disappointment. "Oh Roger, he map hang. I t'ink he wen flunk da test." (2) Double chin.

MASS DROP Facial expression signifying surprise or upset. "My mass wen drop when Doris told me I get stink-breat'!"

MASS DROP EN MASSE

MAUI WOWIE Heavy-duty Valley Isle smokes.

MEAN OUT (1) Difficult; intense. "Wow, da tes' MEAN OUT! Bus' mah brain!" Choice. "Wow, yo' cah MEAN OUT!"

MEMPACHI EYES (mem PAH chee)
  Bambucha eyes, like da fish get.

MENTO Mental. "Wow, Mento! Kaneohe wen
  let you out o' wot?"

ME'UFU (may OO foo) Mahu from Tonga.

MENTO

MIDDLE COMB Major requirement for becoming a surfer. Also **MIDDLE PART**.

MINAHS Minors. No beeg t'ing.

MOCHI CRUNCH

MO' GARAN DAN DA ODDAH ONE Dis mo' bettah dan dat, brah.

MOCHI (MOE chee) Japanese rice patty.

MOCHI CRUNCH Crunchy Japanese rice patty.

MOCHI MAN Japanese version of MACHO MAN. See also SAMURAI.

MOCKET "What, you going Stah Mocket o' wot?"

MOKEMOBILE Local transportation. VW bug with surf racks and many personal adornments, like fuzzy dice or feathers, re-covered seats, souped-up engine, mags, headahs, an' li'dat.

MOKEMOBILE

MONKS FOOD Chinese spaghetti with peanuts and tree fungus. No joke!

MOSHIMOSHI (moe shee MOE shee) How Japanese people answer the phone.

MUFF, MUFFY Real panty-kine guy.

MUFFLER BURNS Diamond Head or
   Tantalus battle scars.

NAAHHH SAD Tired, dry. "Harold told you his new joke? You laugh?" "Naahhh, sad, but!"

I DON'T THINK THAT'S SUCH A GOOD IDEA... LET'S NOT DO THAT.

Haole

NEVAH!!

Local

NEVAH Didn't, don't. HAOLE: "I don't want to do that." LOCAL: "I nevah like!"

NO? Yeah?

NO-BODDAH TIME Pidgin for "Do Not Disturb."

NO-BODDAH TIME

NO GET WISE, BUBBLE EYES, CUT YOU DOWN PEANUT SIZE No make
hi-makamaka o' I goin' slap yo' head.

NO HOM
(no HAWM)
No worry;
take it easy.

NO HOM

NO LIE, RICE EYE

NO LAUGH ME No make fun.

NO LIE You know what this means.

NO LIE, RICE EYE No gimme shibai, Japanee. See also WHAT YOU SAID, BUDDAHEAD?

NO MAKE Stop that! Short for NO MAKE LI'DAT.

NO 'NUFF Insufficient supply. "Can have mo' rice?" "Cannot! No 'nuff!"

NO SKED

NO SKED Don't be afraid.

NUHA (NEW ha) (1) Bent out of shape.
"Wow, what, you all nuha?"
(2) Examacited. "Angie was all NUHA when he wen call her fo' go da Police concert!"

OBAKE (oh BAH kay) (1) Ghost. (2) Kalakoa kine ant'urium.

OBAKE

OHANA

OMAHGOONESS (oh mah GOO ness) Old kine way fo' say CHEE!

OH WOW LI'DAT! How rude! How dare!

OHANA (oh HA na) Family, or just like family.

OLO-OLOS (oh lo OH lohz) Another way to say ALA-ALAS.

OLOPOP (OH lo pop) How you say POPOLO when there's one around.

OMEKO (oh MAY ko) Buddahead fufuna.

ON DA RUN Run away from home.

ON DA RUN

ONLY (OH nee) Really. HAOLE: "That's so unbelievable!" LOCAL: "Wow, on'y trippy!"

OPAE (oh PIE) Small-kine shrimp, either ocean kine or land kine.

OPALA (oh PA la) What you take out twice a week so the opala man can pick 'um up.

OPEN DA LIGHT/CLOSE DA LIGHT
Turn on da light/turn off da light.

OPUS

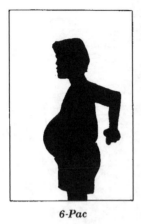

6-Pac

Case

Keg

OPU (OH poo) Place to hold beer.

OTOT (oh TOHT) Filipino fut.

"P" (PEE) Mahu slang for real pretty, real cute. "Oh, she so P, yeah?" Also P-ella: shahp to da max.

PAKAJUNK

PAKAJUNK (pa ka JUNK) Ol' bus' up cah: one fifty-t'ree chevalay, get no mo' front fendah, doah handle no work, glass stay cracked, da trunk stay tied down, blankets on top da seats, get one puka inside da floah fo' littah, get bubble gum in da rus' spots. Still run, but.

PAKIKE (pa KEY kay) (1) Hard, tough. "So stubborn, dat pakike head!" (2) Tight, manini. One Chang is one pakike pake.

PANCIT (pon SEET) P.I. chop suey.

PAO DOCE (pan DOOSS) Portagee sweet bread. Good fo' eat o' fo' fundraisah.

PAPA'A (pa PA'ah) Burnt.

PAPA'A

PARALLEL (pair ah LEL) When somebody
   wen punch you out an' you stay taking one
   nap on da floor.

PARK AN' RUSH Waialae Drive-In without
   da movies.

PEHEA OE? (pay hay ah OH ay) How you
   stay? Appropriate reply is "Maika'i fine!"
   Also PEHEA KO PIKO.

PEKECK (peh KEK) To brok'. "No play wit'
   my toys o' going PEKECK!"

the porkhashe look

PEPEIAO a la Jordache

PEPEIAO
(pay pay OW)
Chinese
designer foods.

PEPEIAO KULI
(pay pay ow
KOO lee)
Deaf ear.

PIKO (PEE ko) Mini-crater in da opu.

PILIPINO (pee lee PEE no) Filipino referring to himself.

PIKO

PILUT (pee LOOT) (1) Polluted, like dirty.
"Oh wow, da watah at Rises all PILUT!"
(2) Polluted, like drunk. "Wayne wen tank
fifty-t'ree beers las' night! He stay so
PILUT!"

PIO (PEE oh) To extinguish. "PIO da bud!"
Also pronounced PEEL. "Peel da light! I
tryin' fo' be romantic!"

POHO (po HO) Lazy; good for nothing.

POKE SQUID To scoah.
   "What, Rory — you wen
   poke squid las' night?"
   If you one girl, no read dis.

POUND Old plantation
   pidgin for WEIGH.
   "Doctah, you
   can pound
   my baby?"

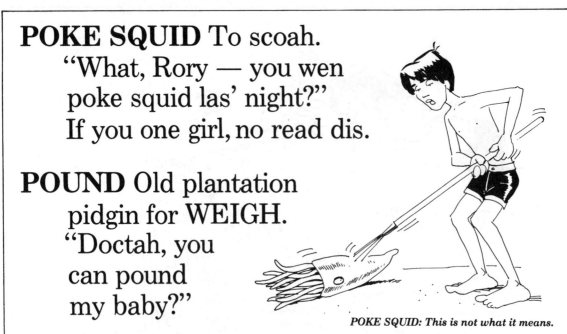

POKE SQUID: This is not what it means.

POUNDAH (1) Big, perfect wave.
   (2) Mountain dove. Da BEEG kine.

OH WOW...
POUNDAH!

POUNDAH

PORTAGEE SHTRAIGHT In poker, when you get one ace, deuce, t'ree, fo' li'dat, but all different colors.

POWAH SURF (1) Places get heavy surf, like Banzai Pipeline or Gas Chambers. (2) Da kine surfing you gotta do in dose kine places.

PROMISE? You really going delivah?

PSS, PSS Mating call of the Waipahu Bukbuk.

PROMISE?

PUA TING (poo ah TEENG) Poor thing, yeah?

PUFF YO' NOSE Plantation pidgin for "Blow yo' nose." What you do when hanakuso say, "Hello! I ready fo' come out."

PUA TING

PUKA HEAD (POO ka head) Someone who get hard time fo' t'ink 'cause he get breeze blowing t'rough hees head.

PUKA PANTS Boroboro pants; natural air conditioning.

Pulehu Chicken *Pulehu Ulua* *Pulehu Dog* *Pulehu Crab*

PULEHU (poo LAY who) Take anything that's raw and dead, throw it in the fire, wait until black and crispy, pull 'em out. Das' PULEHU! (Not really pulehu unless accompanied by plenny cold beer.)

PULL DOWN (poo DOWN) Howzit! Lose weight, eh? See also PUT ON.

PULL DOWN

PUNA BUDS, PUNA BUTTER (POO nah)
Mean out pakalolo from Puna. Sweet, but!

PUNI (POO nee) Lie. "No puni!" Also
PUNIALA.

PUT (PUTT) Otot.

PUT ON Howzit? Gain weight, eh? See also
PULL DOWN.

RAP HEES HEAD/RAP YO' HEAD
Closed-fist version of SLAP YO' HEAD.

RAT BITE (1) Muffler burn. (2) When yo' moddah wen cut yo' hair at home an' she keep missing da hair.

RAT BITE

RES' No ac'! Also TAKE A RES' OR EY, RES'!

RICE EYE Local Oriental. See NO LIE, RICE EYE.

RIGHT ON POPCO'N Garans ballbarans.

HAWAIIAN ROACHES

RIPPAH (One noddah meaning from da oddah book.) Really habuts. "You saw Dahlene aftah George wen stand her up? She was RIPPAH OUT!!"

ROACH, HAWAIIAN Mo' beeg dan da Mainlan' kine. An' dey FLY!

RUBBAH-BAND LEGS Long legs like one popolo. Stretch fah.

RUN SPEED LIMIT

RUBBAH SLIPPAH Da kine you step in
da mud, suction, eh? Da t'ing go brok'!
Hahd fo' fix, yeah?

RUN SPEED LIMIT (1) To go fast. (2) To
do anything really fast.

RUNATE (RUN ah tay) Martial art for
panty guys.

SACKATARY The one who always ends up washing the coffee cups.

SACKATARY

SAFE Real nerd. Da guy who like K.A. da teachah. "Oh dat Renton! He so SAFE!! Make me bahf!"

SAMOAN FAMILY CAR Old auctioned blue-and-white cop car. (Somebody else sent this in. We nevah write 'em!)

SAMURAI Macho man, Japanese style. No say notting when huhu, jus' give stink-eye. See also MOCHI MAN.

Samurai Method of Requesting More Rice.

SCABBING Cruising. Easier fo' do when you get mirror sunglasses.

SCABBING

SCAHF OUT Grind to da max. "No wondah she so momona! She always SCAHF OUT!"

SCOAH (1) To get something really good. "Wow, dis bento so ONO! Scoah, yeah?" (2) Poke squid.

SCRAP Beef. "What, scrap now?"

SHAHKBAIT

SHA! LIMU DAT JOKE! (SHA pronounced two ways: SHAW or SHAA, rhymes with BAA) Laters wit' dat joke. Tired.

SHAHKBAIT White skin on da beach make good kaukau fo' da shahks.

SHI-SHI (SHEE shee) What little old Japanese ladies say when they have to go benjo.

SHOOT

SHOOT! All right! Of coss! "You like manapua, Winton?" "SHOOT! I grind 'um!" Also SHOOTS.

SIDE COMB
Surfah haircut modified for job-hunting.

SINCE WHEN?

SINCE WHEN? HAOLE: "You're obviously not of legal age." LOCAL: "Since when you go bars?"

SINGLE EYE
Rice eye.
See also
DOUBLE EYE.

SKEG

SKEG (1) Surfboard attachment. (2) What you do when you're riding a wave and you drop in on somebody and they want to brok' yo' face. (3) To brok'.

SLAP YO' HEAD
Slap your head.

SLAP YO' HEAD

SLOP MAN
Da little ol' man who come fo' pick up yo' leftovahs fo' take 'um to da peeg fahm.

SMALL PETOOT
(small pee TOOT) Itty-bitty.

SMELL,
LONG TIME NO
Good to see you. "Ey brah, long time no smell!"

SMALL PETOOT

SMELL, SAME Same t'ing. "Wow, Ken. Why you brought white bread when I wen ask you fo' bring da wheat kine?" "Ey, same smell!"

SO DES' KA

SO DES' KA? Really?

SO? T'ROW PAHTY?'' Wow. Big deal. See also LIKE MEDAL?

SO? T'ROW PAHTY?

SOAH Itai.

SPEED RACER (speed RAY sah) (1) Pedal to the metal. (2) What you do when you gotta go. "You saw Dahlene aftah we wen put da Ex-Lax in her chocolate shake? She wen make SPEED RAYSAH!"

SPEED RAYSAH

SQUID Japanee nerd. Very insulting. Means you uji like one squid.

STEADY RIP Da kine B.S. so good, you wanna keep listening to it. "Dat Michael! He always give da teachah one steady rip!"

SUCK FACE

STINK-EAR Only hear the bad stuff.

SUCK FACE Liplock. "I saw you wit' Derek las' night! SUCK FACE TO DA MAX!"

SUK-SUK (sook SOOK) Kinda nasty, but wonderful activity. "Like mek suk-suk?"

SUMMAH FUN
If you bad during school year you get summah school. If you good, you get Summah Fun. See also CHICKEN FAT.

SUMMAH FUN

SWIPE Pineapple moonshine. Intense kine. Can only get at local luaus.

TAKO (TAH ko) What local people call squid so they can use the word squid for other things.

TANKAH (1) Surfboard that seats 6.
(2) Somebody who can tank da beers.

TANKAHS

TANTALUS Das' where dey hold da helicoptah races. Often the scene of MUFFLER BURNS.

360/280 Special numbers signifying high-speed person. "Wow, he go 280 when he talk, yeah?"

TOE JAMS

TILAPIA (tah LOP ee ah) (1) Ete fish. (2) Ete person.

TOE JAMS Hauna feet.

TOTAL OUT

TOFF Tough. Suffah, mine bettah dan yawz.

TOJO (TOE joe) What you call Armando Asuncion when he starts going steady with Mitzi Fujikawa.

TOO MACHI GOOD (too mah chee GOOOOD) Too good, you! Some plenny good. What bachans always say. Also TOO MACHI GURU, TOO MACHI GURU ROOKING.

TOTAL OUT To da max. All da way and then some.

TOWNIE

TOWNIE Insulting term used by people who don't live in town. Means anyone from a Honolulu school.*

TRIP (1) Haole vacation. "Let's go on a trip, honey!" (2) Samoan problem. "Ey, wha's yo' trip?"

*Especially Kaimuki, Roosevelt or McKinley, and especially if they're Japanese who wear Angels Flights, Aloha Shirt tucked in with belt, cute but not as cute as they think, or if they're a girl, nice perm, bleached hair, always dressed very well, big earrings, packed-on makeup, scotch tape on their eyes, and oh yeah, they all drive Cutlasses or Toyota Celicas or Corolla SR-5's.

T'ROW ME OFF

TRIPPING When you going out with somebody but not ready to go steady. "Dennis gave you ring o'wot?" "Nah, on'y tripping."

T'ROW ME OFF Make me lose my train of thought. "No talk so much, you going t'row me off!"

T'ROW OILS Steady rip, you! Getting slippery in heah!

TRUE BOOL: McKinley

TRUE BOOL: Waianae

TRUE BOOL: Waipahu

TRUE BOOL Tried, tested and proven bool of da school.

TRY CRUISE Res'!

TUFF KUKAE You know what this means. An' tuff kukae if you don't!

TUNE To use a part of someone else's body as a musical instrument. "Ey brah, I going tune yo' okole."

UFU (OO foo) Frizzy kine hair. "You saw Mary? She wen ufu her hair to da max! She look like one popolo!"

UKU BILLION, UKU BLUR, UKU MILLION, UKU PILE, UKU PLENTY Plenty.

WHAT DENISE'S SECRET?

UKUBILLION KLEENEX!

UKUBILLION

WAHINE SICK Old plantation pidgin for social disease.

WASE TIME (wayss TIME) Good for nothing. "Wase time, you put makeup!"

WASE TIME

WHAT, SNAPPING?

WASSAMATTAYOU What's your problem?

WERT' Wort'less. "You saw dat movie? Was WERT', man!"

WHANG YO' JAWS Wop yo' jaw.

WHAT, SNAPPING? Are you having a mental problem?

WHAT, WHY? What you say before you ask a rhetorical question. Like for instance, "What, why? I look like one dummy to you?" OR: "What, why? Boddah you?" Also WOW, WHAT?

WHAT YEAR YOU GRAD? How old are you?

WHAT YOU SAID, BUDDAHEAD? Whatcho yo' trip, Nip? See also NO LIE, RICE EYE.

WHODAGUY? Who is that unfamiliar person?

Why don't you go ahead?   I'll come later.

YEAH, NO? That's right, yeah?

YOU GO, I GO STAY COME HAOLE: "Why don't you go ahead to the hotel with everybody else, I'll stay here for a minute and meet you soon." LOCAL: "You go, I go stay come."

YOU NO NEEZ KNOW!!

MOMMY AND DADDY *BUSY?* WHAT DEY *DOING?*

YOU NO NEEZ KNOW

YOU KNOW DA RULES Shut up and get in line.

YOU NO NEEZ KNOW None of your business.

ZAGALAGA (zah gah LAH gah) Junkalunka or jagalaga.

ZEEPY'S (ZEE peez) Wheah you go fo' grind afta da movie or da disco. Zip-pac headquartahs.

ZEEPY'S